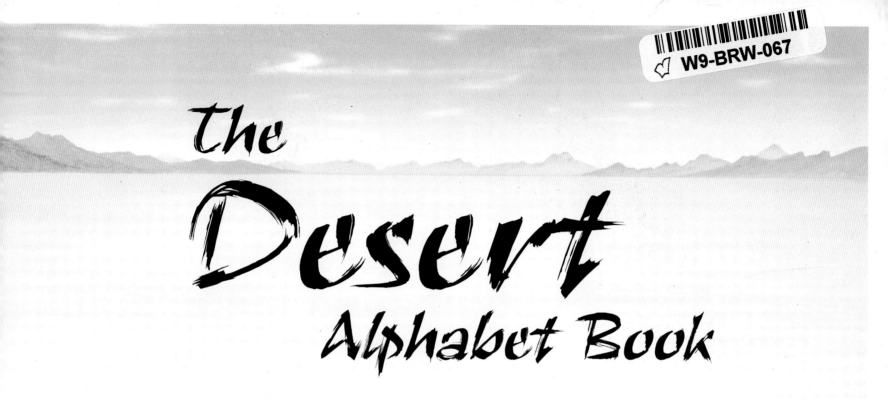

The Desert Alphabet Book

Jerry Pallotta   Illustrated by Mark Astrella

Charlesbridge

Thank you to Joe Martinez, Greg Oshel, and Brian Cassie.

Thank you to all the elementary school kids in California from Ridgecrest, China Lake, Inyokern, Edwards Air Force Base, Lake Los Angeles, and Apple Valley, who told me to write a desert book.
—Jerry Pallotta
Peggotty Beach, 1994

Thank you to Ralph "Icky Bug Man" Masiello for introducing me to Jerry Pallotta.
—Mark Astrella

Published by Charlesbridge
85 Main Street, Watertown, MA 02472
(617) 926-0329
www.charlesbridge.com

Printed in Korea
(hc) 10 9 8 7 6 5 4 3 2 1
(sc) 10 9 8 7 6 5 4 3 2 1

Library of Congress Cataloging-in-Publication Data
Pallotta, Jerry.
    The desert alphabet book / by Jerry Pallotta; illustrated by Mark Astrella.
        p.   cm.
    ISBN-13: 978-0-88106-473-5; ISBN-10: 0-88106-473-4 (reinforced for library use)
    ISBN-13: 978-0-88106-472-8; ISBN-10: 0-88106-472-6 (softcover)
1. Desert biology—Juvenile literature.
2. English language—Alphabet—Juvenile literature. [1. Alphabet.
2. Desert biology.] I. Astrella, Mark, ill. II. Title.
QH88.P34 1994
574.909'54 — dc20
[E]   93-42651

Deserts are areas of earth that get hardly any rain. Usually, deserts get less than ten inches of rain per year. However, thousands of plants and animals live in the desert and have developed unique ways to survive.

A a

A is for Australian Water-holding Frog. How could a frog live in the desert? When it rains, the Australian Water-holding Frog absorbs as much water as it can. Then it buries itself underground and secretes a protective coating around its skin and waits for it to rain again.

B b

B is for Bactrian Camel. This double-humped camel is found in the rocky, cold desert of northern China and Mongolia, the Gobi Desert. It is also called a Shaggy Camel because it has such long fuzzy fur.

It is time for a chat. If you think that all desert creatures are dull-looking and ugly, you might be wrong.

C is for Crimson Chat. The colorful Crimson Chat flies all over the Australian deserts looking for water. What a beautiful bird! Did you know that ninety percent of Australia is desertlands?

Cc

D d

D is for Dromedary Camel. These one-humped camels have been called the "ships of the desert." For thousands of years, people have been using these camels to transport goods from one place to another.

Remember, a Bactrian Camel has two humps like the capital letter B. A Dromedary Camel has one hump like the capital letter D. Luckily, there is no five-humped camel because we would have no capital letter to compare it to!

Maybe someday this book will be delivered by camel to a child who lives in the desert and loves to read.

E e

E is for Elf Owl. The Elf Owl is the smallest owl in the world. Elf Owls eat mostly insects, centipedes, and scorpions. They rip the stinger off before feeding a scorpion to the baby Elf Owls. Elf Owls are found in the Sonoran Desert in the southwest United States.

F f

F is for Fennec.
The Fennec is a small fox. It lives in the deserts
of northern Africa and Arabia. The Fennec spends the
hot day in its underground den where it is cooler. The soles
of its feet are covered with hair so it can walk on the hot sand.

G g

G is for Golden Wheel Spider. Who invented the wheel? Was it people like us? Maybe not. The Golden Wheel Spider curls itself into a ball and rolls down the sand dunes to escape anything that tries to bother it. It is also called a Cartwheeling Spider.

H h

Can you do a cartwheel?

Can you stand on your head?

H is for Headstanding Beetle.
When the ocean fog rolls into the
Namib Desert of Africa, this beetle
has learned to get water by standing
on its head. The fog collects on its body
and the droplets of water slide into its mouth.
This fog-drinking beetle is amazing!

I is for Inland Taipan. This poisonous desert snake has more venom than any other snake on earth. If the Inland Taipan bites you, just say good-bye.

I i

J j

Here is a word
you may not have heard.
It's not a reptile
and not a bird.
This cute desert rodent
is called a Jird!

J is for Jird.

OK, who is the wise guy that
put poetry in this book?

K k

K is for Kulan. Kulans have incredible endurance. People have seen them run without stopping for more than twenty miles. They could easily run a marathon. Kulans are not only found in the desert. They are also found in areas called steppes. A steppe is a huge grassland or plain often found on the edge of a desert.

How many miles are in a marathon?
The alphabet is a clue.

L l

L is for Livingstone.
These cactus plants survive
in the desert by looking like rocks.
They are camouflaged cactuses. They
are called "living stones." These plants have
found a clever way to protect themselves.

M m

M is for Meerkat. Meerkats have learned how to survive by working together as a team. Every Meerkat has a job. They take turns hunting, landscaping, housekeeping, and being on guard. If any trouble is sensed, the guard yells and all the other Meerkats scamper into their tunnels.

N is for Namaqua Sandgrouse. There are many different species of sandgrouse in the Sahara Desert. The Namaqua Sandgrouse flies to a watering hole and submerges its breast feathers. When it flies back to its nest, the chicks drink from the wet feathers.

Nn

O is for Oasis. An Oasis is an area in the desert that has a continuous supply of freshwater. The water could be from a well, a spring, or maybe an underground aquifer. An Oasis is always a welcome sight to a thirsty desert traveler.

O o

P p

P is for Palmate Gecko. Usually web-footed creatures live near water. This lizard has webbed feet and lives in the desert. The Palmate Gecko uses its webbed feet to dig in the sand. Having webbed feet is easier than carrying a shovel!

Watch out, Gecko! Something sneaky has its eyes on you!

Q q

Q is for Quail Thrush. If you are a bird-watcher, you might have to look carefully to see a Quail Thrush. The colors of its feathers blend in with the ground. This Quail Thrush has a spicy name. It is called a Cinnamon Quail Thrush.

Time out!
This book is dry.
Maybe it is too dry.
This book needs some
RAIN!

Mount Wai-ale-ale in
Kauai, Hawaii, is the place
with the most rainy days.
It rains about three
hundred and fifty days per
year. Bring an umbrella!

R r **R** is for Red Racer. The Red Racer is a Coachwhip snake that lives in the Mojave Desert. It is a favorite of kids who live in the area. The Red Racer moves fast and bites, but it is not poisonous.

S is for Saguaro. The Saguaro is the largest and tallest cactus in the world. Cactuses are plants that are called succulents. Succulents store water. The Saguaro is also a tree—it has a wooden frame inside. The Saguaro is one of the slowest growing plants. After ten years, a Saguaro is only about six inches tall.

S s

T t

T is for Tortoise.
Actually, this is a Desert Tortoise.
A Tortoise is a land turtle. This
turtle eats flowers and other desert
plants to get moisture. The deserts
are home to some of the prettiest
wildflowers on earth. A desert book would
not be complete without mentioning wildflowers.

U is for Ursine Giant Skipper. There are more than twenty thousand butterfly species in the world. Some of them live in the desert. The caterpillar of the Ursine Giant Skipper escapes the scorching desert heat by burrowing inside the roots of the yucca plant.

Uu

V v

V is for Vaquira. In the United States, these desert-dwelling, pig-like mammals are called Collared Peccaries. In Mexico, they are called Javelinas but in some South American countries they are called Vaquiras. When traveling, they walk in single file.

This frog looks awfully familiar.
The Water-holding Frog is still
underground waiting for rain.

During winter,
some animals become
inactive and go into a deep sleep
called hibernation. When a creature
becomes inactive to escape heat,
it is called estivation. Look! This frog
has been estivating since the A page!
The sound of raindrops will wake this frog up.

W w

W is for Welwitschia. This remarkable plant can live for as long as two thousand years. It looks dead but it isn't. The whole plant is actually two leaves that keep splitting and growing.

X is for Xerus. This squirrel does not even think about climbing trees. It is a ground squirrel. The Xerus has learned to shade itself with its tail.

Xx

Y y

Y is for Yardang. A Yardang is a desert landform. It was eroded by wind and sand. It is also called a column, a pinnacle, or a spire. Some other desert landforms are sand dunes, mesas, buttes, playas, dry lake beds, arroyos, salt flats, and desert pavement.

Z z

Z is for Zaita. Most plants cannot live in salty soil but the Zaita is a "salt lover." It sucks salt up through its roots and stems. The salt then dries on its leaves and looks like fallen snow. Scientists think the salt reflects light and heat and, therefore, cools the plant.

There are a zillion ways to survive in the desert. The Zaita has developed a unique way to survive.

Is it a mirage? No, it's dessert! Many people get dessert and desert mixed up. It is easy to remember that dessert has two S letters, just like strawberry shortcake. This is not strawberry shortcake. This is an ice cream sundae with whipped cream, hot fudge, nuts, jimmies, and a cherry on top.